Christmas 2014

To Ava.

From Grandma

Merry Christmas

COMFORT DOGS

by Natalie Lunis

Consultant: Mr. Tim Hetzner
President of Lutheran Church Charities and Founder of the LCC K-9
Comfort Dog Ministry

BEARPORT
PUBLISHING

New York, New York

Publisher: Kenn Goin
Editorial Director: Adam Siegel
Creative Director: Spencer Brinker
Design: Dawn Beard Creative
Photo Researcher: Picture Perfect Professionals, LLC

Library of Congress Cataloging-in-Publication Data

Lunis, Natalie.
  Comfort dogs / by Natalie Lunis.
    pages cm — (Dog heroes)
  Audience: Age 7–12.
  Includes bibliographical references and index.
  ISBN-13: 978-1-62724-287-5 (library binding)
  ISBN-10: 1-62724-287-2 (library binding)
  1. Animals—Therapeutic use—Juvenile literature. 2. Human-animal relationships—Juvenile literature. I. Title.
  RM931.A65L86 2015
  615.8'5158—dc23
                        2014012773

For more information, write to Bearport Publishing Company, Inc., 45 West 21st Street, Suite 3B, New York, New York 10010. Printed in the United States of America.

10 9 8 7 6 5 4 3 2 1

Table of Contents

Torn Apart by a Tornado

At the end of May 2013, Moore, Oklahoma, was **shattered**. A powerful tornado had ripped through the town, killing 25 people and injuring nearly 400. Thousands of homes and businesses had been destroyed. The 200-mile-per-hour (322 kph) winds had even left the local elementary school in ruins.

The tornado approaching Moore, Oklahoma

After the terrible disaster, teams started arriving from around the state as well as from around the country. Some brought much-needed supplies, such as food, clothing, and blankets. Others set up **shelters** for people who were suddenly homeless. One group, made up of **handlers** and their dogs, was prepared to offer a different kind of help. Its mission was to bring **comfort** to people who were hurting **emotionally** because they had lost so much.

Rescuers searched for survivors after the tornado had passed.

The tornado that struck Moore and the surrounding area was one of the worst in U.S. history.

"Please Pet Me"

The dogs and handlers who arrived in Oklahoma were part of the **Lutheran** Church **Charities** (LCC) K-9 Comfort Dog program. They knew just what to do, since all of them had already traveled to places where people were facing a **crisis**. In fact, two of the dogs that came to Oklahoma, Louie and Jackson, had experience helping out after a tornado. Two years earlier, in May 2011, they had spent time providing comfort to survivors in Joplin, Missouri, after a huge tornado struck the town.

LCC K-9 Comfort Dogs and their handlers in Moore, Oklahoma

The LCC K-9 Comfort Dog program is based in Addison, Illinois. The comfort dogs travel to a community that needs their help when they are invited by a local church.

During their stay in Oklahoma, the comfort dogs kept up with a busy schedule. They visited badly damaged neighborhoods, shelters where homeless families were staying, and hospitals where injured people were being treated. Wherever they went, they wore the official LCC K-9 Comfort Dog "uniform"—a blue vest with the words "Please Pet Me" printed on it.

Volunteers who work with the LCC K-9 Comfort Dog program say that the dogs are a great help to both children and adults.

Bringing Comfort

Petting a furry, friendly dog may seem like a simple act. However, handlers and others who work with comfort dogs know that many good things happen when people spend time with these gentle, loving animals. This is especially true for people who are going through a difficult time, such as the **aftermath** of a tornado or other **natural disaster**.

Comfort dogs meeting with survivors of the tornado that hit Moore, Oklahoma

Tim Hetzner, one of the leaders of the LCC K-9 Comfort Dog program, has seen how people respond to the dogs many times. "As they keep petting the dogs, we see smiles come onto their faces," he explains. "They start feeling like they'll get through this and they will be okay. Yes, there was loss, but we will grow through that and be stronger."

Scientific research has shown that petting a dog is good for a person's health. It causes blood pressure to go down, which is good for the heart and other parts of the body.

Furry Counselors

Being with a soft, gentle dog can help a person feel calmer and more peaceful. However, that's not the only way that comfort dogs can help. The dogs can also make it easier for people to talk about their feelings and then feel better as a result.

Many people think that dogs have a natural sense of empathy. That means that they understand and are able to feel what people are feeling.

A counselor is a person whose job it is to help people in tough situations understand their feelings so they can heal. Program leader Tim Hetzner has said that the dogs are like furry counselors.

This is what happened when some LCC K-9 Comfort Dogs visited Walther Lutheran High School in Melrose Park, Illinois, in 2010. Students were sad and upset because a boy from the school had died in a drowning accident. One of the boy's friends was especially sad. After a comfort dog walked over and put its head in the boy's lap, the boy was finally able to express his feelings. He cried and then talked about the loss of his friend.

Comfort dogs visiting students at Walther Lutheran High School

The Start of an Idea

The LCC K-9 Comfort Dog program started in 2008 as a response to two terrible events. One was Hurricane Katrina, which hit New Orleans in August 2005. The deadly hurricane caused enormous flooding, destroyed thousands of homes, and killed more than 1,800 people. In the days and weeks after the hurricane, program leader Tim Hetzner and others noticed how much people cared about their pets. Some owners even risked their lives trying to keep their animals safe.

Hurricane Katrina destroyed buildings all along the coast of Louisiana, Mississippi, and Alabama. This photo shows flooding in Baton Rouge, Louisiana.

    The other tragedy was a shooting on a college campus in Illinois in February 2008. Five people were killed and twenty-one were injured as a result. Lutheran Church Charities brought comfort dogs to help people afterward. The dogs were in fact a great comfort to those they spent time with, and the group realized that the "furry counselors" could help lots more people.

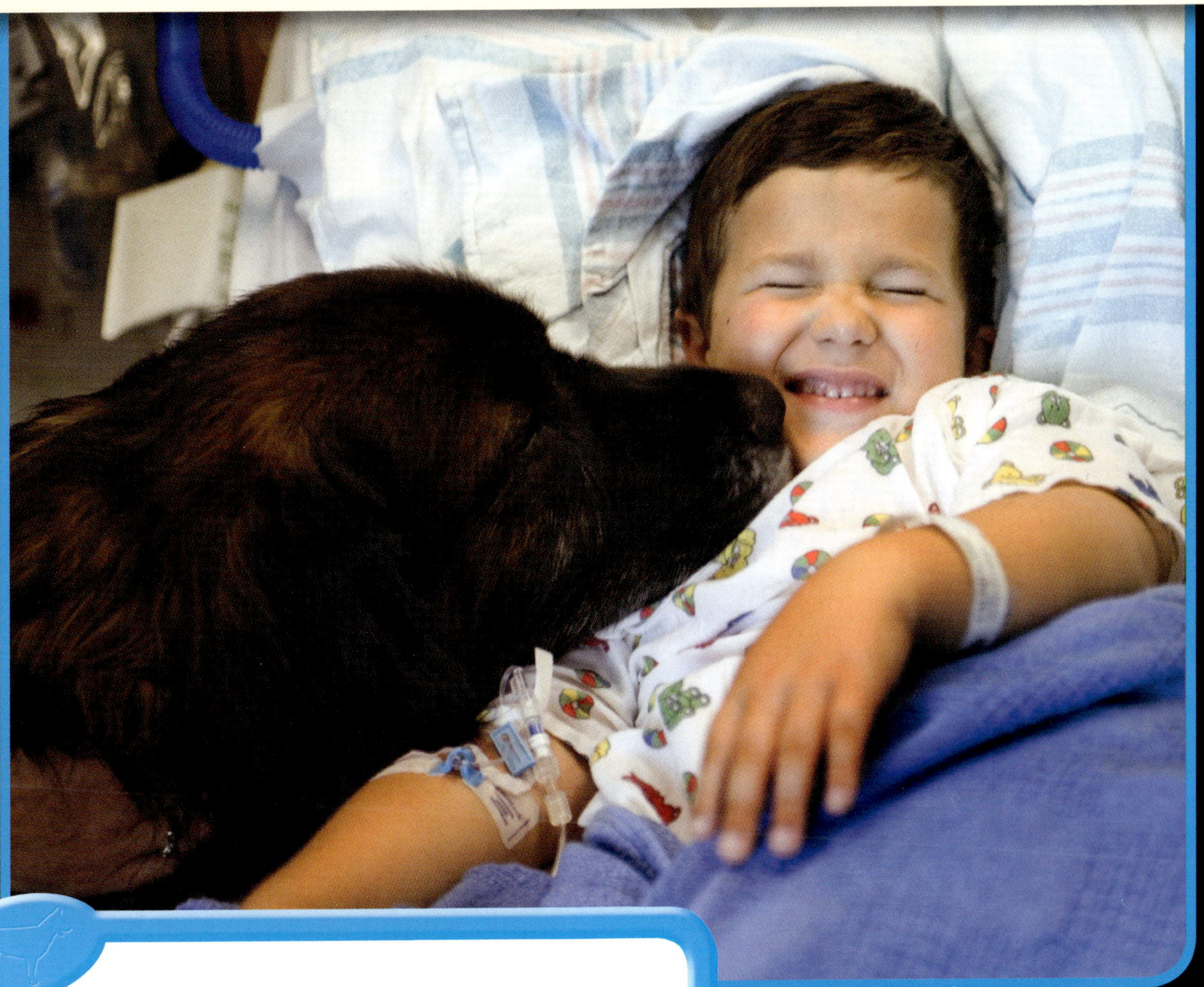

This therapy dog is visiting a young patient in a hospital.

When dogs and other animals, together with their handlers, visit people in order to help them emotionally, it's called animal-assisted therapy. The dogs are often called **therapy dogs**.

Meet the Dogs

All the LCC K-9 Comfort Dogs are golden retrievers. Today, there are more than 80 dogs based in sixteen different states. Each one belongs to a Lutheran school or **congregation** and lives with a family in the school or church community.

A comfort dog is a very special kind of therapy dog. LCC K-9 Comfort Dogs and their handlers are prepared to respond to people who are hurting because of crisis situations.

Why does the group use only golden retrievers? There are several reasons why this **breed** is suited for the job of being a comfort dog. Golden retrievers are intelligent and easy to train. They are also generally gentle and friendly. Even someone who might sometimes be afraid of dogs would be unlikely to be scared of one of these big, kind-hearted **canines**.

Because of its friendly personality, the golden retriever is one of the most popular breeds of dogs in the United States.

Time for Training

An LCC K-9 Comfort Dog needs to have a friendly, easy-going personality. However, that's not all a dog needs to travel around the country with a handler and meet new people. Becoming a comfort dog takes months of training, too.

Dogs who are just starting out are known as "comfort dogs in training." As part of its training, this dog is being brought to help out after the tornado in Moore, Oklahoma.

Comfort dogs start their training when they are only eight weeks old.

During their training, the dogs learn many skills. To start out, they work on socialization, which means getting along with other dogs and with all kinds of people, including strangers. Then they move on to learn the special skills they need for the job. For example, to make people feel safe and loved, the dogs learn to bow their heads. To show that they want to feel close, they put their heads in people's laps.

Hooray for Handlers!

Comfort dog handlers also receive plenty of training. They learn many things to help them manage their dogs. Among them are how to help the dogs travel comfortably and how to keep them safe at disaster sites.

Comfort dogs at work

Part of a handler's job is to watch for signs of **fatigue** and **stress** in a dog—especially when helping at disaster sites or in other tough situations. During these times, the handler makes sure the dog has time to rest and relax.

Just as importantly, a handler learns how to respond
to people who need comforting. Sometimes that means
just listening once the person is ready to share his or her
feelings. Sometimes it means helping someone who has
met with a "furry counselor" find a human counselor,
such as a **pastor** or **therapist**, to talk things over with.
By reaching out to others in this way, the dog and its
handler work as a team.

**LCC K-9 Comfort Dogs are known
for being good listeners. Their
handlers are good listeners, too.**

Lifting People's Spirits

Once a comfort dog has completed its training, the dog becomes **certified** to do work. With its handler, it can now go to disaster sites such as Joplin, Missouri, and Moore, Oklahoma. Some of the other hard-hit places the dogs have been invited to include towns in the northeast struck by Hurricane Sandy in October 2012. They have also traveled to West, Texas, where an accidental explosion killed 15 people and injured many others in April 2013.

This comfort dog meets with students in West, Texas.

Communities suffering from disasters are not the only places the dogs travel to, however. They also visit **nursing homes**, hospitals, and **veterans**' organizations. In all these places, the comfort dogs lift people's spirits and help them **cope** with the loneliness or worries that can come with everyday life.

The LCC K-9 Comfort Dogs and their handlers often visit schools and community groups so that people can meet the dogs and learn about their work.

The dogs are the center of attention whenever they visit hospitals.

Big Hugs for First Responders

The dogs that serve with Lutheran Church Charities are not the only canines that are on call to comfort people in times of trouble. Rosie and Clarence are St. Bernards that belong to police officers Lieutenant William Gordon and Sergeant Laura Gordon. These loving canines are ready to help, too.

Clarence and Rosie

The Gordons saw how much help a dog could be when Rosie helped William and other **first responders** deal with the stress that goes with their work. As a result, they started to train more dogs. Today, they run an organization that provides comfort dogs to police officers, firefighters, and other emergency workers. As William jokingly points out, Rosie and Clarence are a new kind of police dog. "These dogs," he says, "all they do is love people."

Police officers William and Laura Gordon are on the police force in Greenfield, Massachusetts. William is shown here visiting a Greenfield classroom with Rosie and telling children about her work.

Rosie and Clarence are the first official police comfort dogs in the United States.

Comfort in the Courtroom

Rosie and Clarence have shown that dogs can bring comfort to people with extremely stressful jobs, such as police officers. Other dogs have proven that they can comfort people who have seen or experienced crimes as well.

Molly B is one of the first dogs in the United States to be specially trained for the job of supporting witnesses and others in the courtroom. She is a Labrador retriever and was trained by the organization Canine Companions for Independence.

The idea of using dogs to offer comfort to young crime **witnesses** is fairly new. However, more and more **district attorney's** offices across the United States are starting to do so.

A large poodle named Reggie works in California
with the Sacramento County district attorney's office.
When children come to the courtroom to be questioned
by lawyers, he sits with them and allows himself to be
petted. According to Tatiana Morfas, who works with the
district attorney's office, Reggie is a big help to children
who must **testify** in court. "Once they connect with
Reggie," she says, "you can see their faces change. He
makes them comfortable and secure in an environment
that can be really scary."

Reggie received special training before becoming a comfort dog for the district attorney's office.

Cool Schools

Where else can gentle, well-behaved dogs bring a calming presence and help people feel better? Students at Tufts University in Medford, Massachusetts, would say that the dogs are a huge help at their school at exam time. During final exam week in December 2013, four dogs visited the Tufts library so that students could spend time petting them and talking to them.

In 2010, Meika (left) and Troy (right) visited students at Tufts University during final exam week.

Everyone who took part in the very special study break reported feeling better as a result. Megan Kiely Mueller, a teacher at Tufts **veterinary school**, said the event "showed how connected people are to animals." At the same time, it showed just one more of the many ways that dogs can bring happiness—or at least a smile—to people in need of comfort.

Some LCC K-9 Comfort Dogs are based at Lutheran schools. They greet students at the beginning and end of the school day. Sometimes they also help out in the guidance counselor's office.

Students at a Lutheran school in Wisconsin snuggle with a comfort dog.

Just the Facts

- Each LCC K-9 Comfort Dog has several handlers assigned to it. Altogether, there are more than 450 handlers who work with the dogs.

- When an LCC K-9 Comfort Dog is placed with a school or church, there is a special ceremony to mark the event. It is called "the passing of the leash."

- One of the jobs of a comfort dog is to help people who are sad because a friend or family member has died. The dogs sometimes attend the funerals so that they can be there for the people who are hurting.

- An LCC K-9 Comfort Dog retires, or stops working, when it is eight to ten years old.

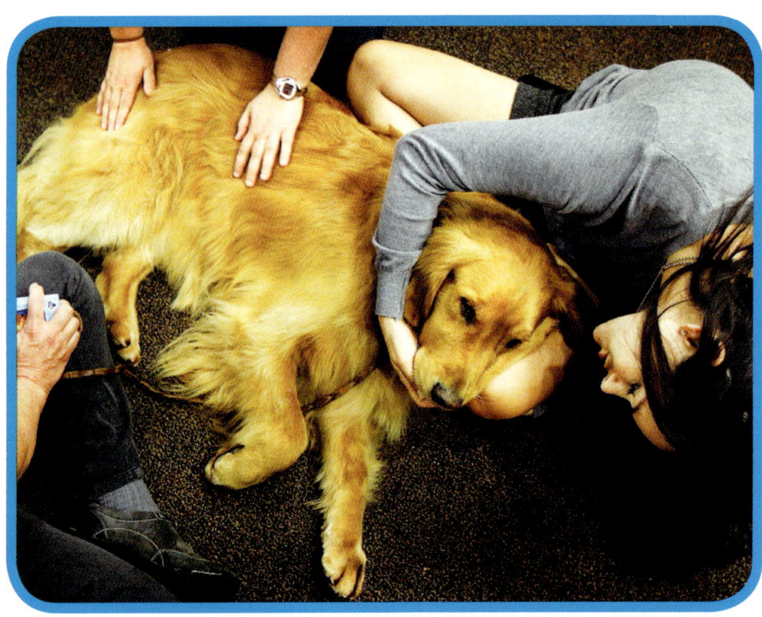

The University of Texas invites dogs in during exam weeks. Students there are happy to give this golden retriever a hug.

COMFORT DOGS

Golden retriever

St. Bernard

Labrador retriever

Standard poodle

aftermath (AF-*tur*-math) the time following an event

breed (BREED) a kind of dog

canines (KAY-nyenz) animals that are members of the dog family

certified (SUR-tuh-fide) having met the official requirements to do a specific job

charities (CHAIR-uh-teez) groups that work to help others

comfort (KUHM-furt) the feeling of being relaxed and free from pain or worry

congregation (*kon*-gruh-GAY-shuhn) a group of people who come together for religious worship

cope (KOHP) to deal with something, such as a problem or situation

crisis (KRYE-siss) an extremely difficult time or problem

district attorney (DIS-trikt uh-TUR-nee) a lawyer who handles cases for the government within a certain part of the state

emotionally (i-MOH-*shuhn*-uh-lee) in a way that has to do with feelings

fatigue (fuh-TEEG) being tired due to hard work

first responders (FURST ri-SPOND-urz) the first people who come to the rescue of someone in trouble

handlers (HAND-lurz) people who train and work with dogs

Lutheran (LOOTH-uh-ruhn) a Christian religious group

natural disaster (NACH-ur-uhl duh-ZASS-tur) an event caused by weather or nature that results in great damage or loss

nursing homes (NUR-sing HOHMZ) places that care for people who are elderly or ill

pastor (PASS-tur) the person who is in charge of a church

shattered (SHAT-urd) broken apart

shelters (SHEL-turz) places that provide safety from danger

stress (STRESS) nervousness, worry

testify (TESS-tuh-fye) to speak in front of other people about something that happened

therapist (THER-uh-*pist*) a counselor; someone who is trained to help others with their worries and problems

therapy dogs (THER-uh-pee DAWGZ) dogs that visit places such as hospitals to cheer up people and make them feel more comfortable

veterans (VET-ur-uhnz) people who have served in the armed forces

veterinary school (VET-ur-uh-*ner*-ee SKOOL) a place where people learn to become animal doctors

witnesses (WIT-nuh-suhz) people who have seen crimes or other events

Bibliography

Andreassi, Katia, and Amanda Fiegl. "After the Bombing, Comfort Dogs Come to Boston." *National Geographic.* April 18, 2013. (http://news.nationalgeographic.com/news/2013/13/130418-boston-marathon-dogs-comfort-newtown/)

Contrada, Fred. "Unique Greenfield Program Uses St. Bernard Dogs to Comfort Police, Firefighters." MassLive. December 6, 2013. (www.masslive.com/news/index.ssf/2013/12/grenfield_police_unveil_comfor.html)

Lutheran Church Charities Web Site (www.k9comfort.org)

Nix, Naomi. "Illinois Comfort Dogs Head to Oklahoma in Wake of Deadly Tornado." *Chicago Tribune.* May 21, 2013. (http://articles.chicagotribune.com/2013-05-21/news/chi-illinois-comfort-dogs-head-to-oklahoma-in-wake-of-deadly-tornado-20130521_1_six-dogs-lutheran-church-charities-joplin)

Zempel, Jill. "K-9 Comfort Dogs." LEA Shaping the Future. Summer 2011. (http://stf.lea.org/summer2011/feat2comfortDogs.html)

Read More

Feldman, Heather. *The Story of the Golden Retriever (Dogs Throughout History).* New York: PowerKids Press (2000).

Lindeen, Mary. *It's a Dog's Life.* North Mankato, MN: Capstone (2012).

Tagliaferro, Linda. *Therapy Dogs (Dog Heroes).* New York: Bearport (2005).

Learn More Online

Visit these Web sites to learn more about comfort dogs:

www.akc.org/breeds/golden_retriever/index.cfm

www.chaps.us.com/aboutus.html

www.k9comfort.org

About the Author

Natalie Lunis has written many nonfiction books for children.
She lives in New York's lower Hudson River Valley.